pocketbooks[08]

Distance & Proximity

Thomas A. Clark

Distance & Proximity

photographs by Olwen Shone

pocketbooks
Morning Star Publications
Polygon
Taigh Chearsabhagh
National Galleries of Scotland

2000

Published by:
pocketbooks
Canongate Venture (5), New Street, Edinburgh, EH8 8BH.

Morning Star Publications
Canongate Venture (5), New Street, Edinburgh, EH8 8BH.

Polygon
22 George Square, Edinburgh, EH8 9LF.

Taigh Chearsabhagh
Lochmaddy, North Uist, Western Isles, HS6 5AA.

National Galleries of Scotland
Belford Road, Edinburgh, EH4 3DS.

Typeset in Minion and Univers.
Typesetting and artworking by Bluelines Media Services.
Design concept by Lucy Richards with Alec Finlay.
Printed and bound by Redwood Books Limited, Trowbridge.
Printed on Munken Elk Print Extra 90gsm available from Trebruk UK Limited.

Published with the assistance of grants from the Scottish Arts Council National
Lottery Fund, the Highlands and Islands Enterprise (HI Arts),

A CIP record is available from the British Library.

ISBN 0 7486 6288X

List of Contents

Acknowledgements

A number of these prose poems have been previously published: 'In Praise of Walking' in *The Unpainted Landscape* (Coracle Press 1987) and reprinted by Cairn Gallery 1988, by Walking Bird Press, Newfoundland 1997, and in *The Tempers Of Hazard* (Paladin 1993); *On Looking at the Sea*, with Elizabeth Ogilvie, by the Mead Gallery, Warwick 1997; *Jouissance*, with James Hugonin, by The Fruitmarket Gallery, Edinburgh 1992; *Of Shade And Shadow*, by Moschatel Press 1992, and in *A Curious Architecture* (Stride 1996); *Riasg Buidhe* with Roger Ackling, by Cairn Gallery 1987, and in *Tormentil & Bleached Bones*, (Polygon 1993).

An exhibition featuring these photographs takes place at Taigh Chearsabhagh (North Uist), from 4 to 31 May 2001. Thomas A. Clark's residency at Taigh Chearsabhagh was funded by the Scottish Book Trust. A retrospective of Moschatel Press, 'Words for the Mantlepiece', will be presented in the The Keillor Library at the Dean Gallery (Edinburgh) 24th February to 29th of April, 2001. We would like to thank Taigh Chearsabhagh and the National Galleries of Scotland for their support as copublishers of *Distance & Proximity*.

We would also like to thank Olwen Shone and Thomas A. Clark; Alison Humphry, Ken Cockburn and Sophy Dale; Cluny Sheeler and Simon Williams at Bluelines Media Services; Lucy Richards; Alison Bowden and Emma Darling at Polygon; The Department of Fine Art, Duncan of Jordanstone College of Art, University of Dundee; Harry Gilonis; Elizabeth James; and Robin Gillanders.

Editor's Preface

The particular qualities of these poems will be familiar to anyone who has ever heard Tom Clark read his work. He has a gift for quiet immediacy, allowing us to consider 'the first of all pleasures . . . that things exist in and for themselves'. His art succeeds by its limitation as he is determined to address only what he knows and has experienced first hand.

The poems emerge from Clark's daily practice of the short walk. Thus *Distance & Proximity* may be considered within the tradition of the walking essays of Hazlitt, Stevenson and Thoreau. Walking is a pursuit available to any of us at any time. It is a political as well as a personal act. Clark invites us to look at the world with attention and to receive in return a form of redemption, a falling away from the self, and a sense of the numinous. If we accept his disavowal of the confessional we can gain much from the mode of receptivity that his poetry makes possible.

This collection brings together a number of pieces previously published by Moschatel Press, which Tom and Laurie Clark run from the Cairn Gallery in Nailsworth. *In Praise of Walking* has already passed through numerous editions, and has come to stand as something of a credo. Here Clark's poems find a kinship with the suggestive textures of Olwen Shone's photographs. We are delighted to have the opportunity to present here the work of such a gifted young photographer.

Alec Finlay

In Praise of Walking

Early one morning, any morning, we can set out, with the least possible baggage, and discover the world.

It is quite possible to refuse all the coercion, violence, property, triviality, to simply walk away.

That something exists outside ourselves and our preoccupations, so near, so readily available, is our greatest blessing.

Walking is the human way of getting about.

Always, everywhere, people have walked, veining the earth with paths, visible and invisible, symmetrical and meandering.

There are walks on which we tread in the footsteps of others, walks on which we strike out entirely for ourselves.

A journey implies a destination, so many miles to be consumed, while a walk is its own measure, complete at every point along the way.

There are things we will never see, unless we walk to them.

Walking is a mobile form of waiting.

What I take with me, what I leave behind, are of less importance than what I discover along the way.

To be completely lost is a good thing on a walk.

The most distant places seem most accessible once one is on the road.

Convictions, directions, opinions, are of less importance than sensible shoes.

In the course of a walk, we usually find out something about our companion, and this is true even when we travel alone.

When I spend a day talking I feel exhausted, when I spend it walking I am pleasantly tired.

The pace of a walk will determine the number and variety of things to be encountered, from the broad outlines of a mountain range to a tit's nest among the lichen, and the quality of attention that will be brought to bear upon them.

A rock outcrop, a hedge, a fallen tree, anything that turns us out of our way, is an excellent thing on a walk.

Wrong turnings, doubling back, pauses and digressions, all contribute to the dislocation of a persistent self-interest.

Everything we meet is equally important or unimportant.

The most lonely places are the most lovely.

Walking is egalitarian and democratic; we do not become experts at walking and one side of the road is as good as another.

Walking is not so much romantic as reasonable.

The line of a walk is articulate in itself, a kind of statement.

Pools, walls, solitary trees, are natural halting places.

We lose the flavour of walking if it becomes too rare or too extraordinary, if it turns into an expedition; rather it should be quite ordinary, unexceptional, just what we do.

Daily walking, in all weathers, in every season, becomes a sort of ground or continuum upon which the least emphatic occurrences are registered clearly.

A stick of ash or blackthorn, through long use, will adjust itself to the palm.

Of the many ways through a landscape, we can choose, on each occasion, only one, and the project of the walk will be to remain responsive, adequate, to the consequences of the choice we have made, to confirm the chosen way rather than refuse the others.

One continues on a long walk not by effort of will but through fidelity.

Storm clouds, rain, hail, when we have survived these we seem to have taken on some of the solidity of rocks and trees.

A day, from dawn to dusk, is the natural span of a walk.

A dull walk is not without value.

To walk for hours on a clear night is the largest experience we can have.

For the right understanding of a landscape, information must come to the intelligence from all the senses.

Looking, singing, resting, breathing, are all complementary to walking.

Climbing uphill, the horizon grows wider; descending, the hills gather round.

We can take a walk which is a sampling of different airs: the invigorating air of the heights; the filtered air of a pine forest; the rich air over ploughed earth.

We can walk between two places and in so doing establish a link between them, bring them into a warmth of contact, like introducing two friends.

There are walks on which I lose myself, walks which return me to myself again.

Is there anything that is better than to be out, walking, in the clear air?

On Looking at the Sea

Walking down to the sea, with the hills behind me, with the miles inside me, what lies before me is immense, a glittering and shining expanse, both limit and release.

A slow curve of shell sand, sand of white silica, Torridonian sand or sand of grey basalt; these are the margins, tracts of delay and preparation.

If fate is the fruit of character, what does it mean to come down to the sea?

As bladder wrack will float a stone, contemplation of the horizon brings a perceptible lifting of the centre of gravity.

A stretch of sea can lie between hills like an acre of bluebells in sunshine.

No amount of looking will ever exhaust that which can be taken in at a glance.

Looking is an acknowledgement before any recognition.

A contour in the hills may contain the sea, as the body may be full of loneliness.

The complement to looking is listening, to lie back in the marram grass, with eyes closed, while oystercatcher, redshank and whimbrel call the distances.

Barnacles sing, tangle rots, the summer days are long and inconsequential.

For a brief season, a bewilderment of butterflies, a broadcast of colours, ragwort, clover, tufted vetch, self-heal, eyebright, wild thyme, is steadied by the blue of sea and sky.

Within the idiom of the tide, ripples in sand or the edges of receding waves have the clarity of a statement.

Sand, shells, pebbles, boulders are graded in an order that is always open to revision.

After the gale, a snow or ash of sea-spume, a froth of spent rage, covers everything, a wounded guillemot drags itself over a litter of boulders, in the massive calm before a new front approaches.

There is a darkness in excess of light, a lull in the crash of thought, on a walk beside the flowering blackthorn of the wave.

Above the tideline, an old blue rope is entangled in a bramble bush.

What was looked for in the hills and in the recesses of the forest is found at last in the sea; the transformation of qualities into quantity.

Time lost looking at the sea is precisely loss of time.

On looking at the sea, it is not the sea but the looking that is redemptive.

On some mornings it will take all the blue of the sea to wash the sleep from your eyes.

Where waves were driven as spray over the dunes, a clear water stands in weed-held pools.

Whimbrel, redshank, oystercatcher; all the distances awake echoes.

Every inscription is erased, every direction countered, that it might be the sea, not current, tide or wave, that rests in the gaze that rests upon it.

Every distance has an internal duplicate which can be measured and sustained.

When we are far from the sea, within closed horizons, we can look again and again at its absence.

Jouissance

The first of all pleasures is that things exist in and for themselves.

As light moves over a surface, it lingers here and there, on a branch, a gate, an old wall, as if with affection.

Sometimes, beyond a screen of trees, in a moment out of time, a meadow extends an invitation impossible to resist.

All the profusion of the hedgerow arises from the articulation of a few precise forms.

It is only order that can go beyond itself, only form that one morning can burst into flower.

After rain, the trees seem to breathe more easily, to declare their own shapes more clearly, to be committed even more to the vertical.

Intelligence is not a competence but a brightness.

The knowledge we possess is leaden and useless compared with the knowledge that suddenly arrives, with an energy that burns up every complacency.

As the shape of the winter sun is held in mist and cloud, so joy may be veiled or contained.

From values, shadows, tones, we may learn a tenderness, a fineness of concern, which we can lend in turn to values, shadows, tones.

Without calm, there is no vivacity, without conviction, no repose.

As light and colour are not tied to any object or locality, so an appreciation of colour and light can liberate us from attachment to particular forms.

In small things, delight is intense.

If you take the path through the barley, the beards of the barley will caress your bare arms.

To fall asleep in the marram grass is to have the pleasure of waking in the marram grass.

Over the fields, through the woods, by the stream: the prepositions may work through a greater range of abilities and susceptibilities than the more conspicuous verbs and nouns.

Where a hedge has been laid, a generation ago, the play of light and shadow along the hollow lane is still intelligible.

In the candour of the grass, a new calf is curled up, head tucked into its long legs, in a sleep as simple as its shape.

At the water's edge, where meadowsweet gathers the remaining light, fragrance is released on the air and forms that were limits relax into the grain of dusk.

Enjoyment is a fullness of response to the abundance of the world.

Of Shade And Shadow

The present age has declared war on shadow – with noise, reason, acid rain.

The impulse that began with the clearing of the forest continues in the demand that nothing be withheld, no opinion or confidence, no joy or wound.

Reticence is a kind of shade, the foliage around a sacred grove.

Anything continually on show, anything which does not periodically conceal itself, begins to lose definition, to fade into its surroundings, like old paintwork on a shop front.

If measurement, logic and purpose take their bearings from light, wildness, tenderness, profusion, are some of the gifts of shade.

There is a time to go out, to be dispersed in light, and a time to return again, faculty by faculty, to rest in one's own weight.

We should cherish all forms of delay, of arrestment or digression, any interruption in our incessant light.

As there is a theology of light, so there is a practice of shadows, a poverty of intention, a duplicating and neutralising of forms, a waiting that renounces every path.

The trembling of shadows is contagious.

Once there were civilisations, great articulations of light and shadow, which are now only broken columns in the grass.

Reserve swells towards a ripeness of speech, a fruit which is proffered without reservation.

In every assumption we make, in any energetic movement of thought, we should remember shade, the obscured connections, the mitigating circumstance, the shelter one thing lends to another.

Often where a shadow has parted from the branch, a small scar is left behind.

One thinks of the patience of shadows, but there is also their tension, their immediacy of response.

The longest shadows reach back into childhood.

There are spring days, before the first leaves have appeared, when the light in the beech wood is so strong that sunbeams and shadows appear substantial as beech trunks.

When the sun shines behind the alders, it throws small ovals of light onto the shaded path.

The simplification of form, the inhibition of colour which a subject observes in its own shadow may precipitate the moment when even the shadow will be discarded.

A shadow can be one fact among others or a gap, a tear, a fissure in the continuity of things.

On those days when I find myself in possession of a shadow, I often have the urge to watch it dance.

As a fly in a room can intensify the stillness, shadows draped in a corner will blunt the limits to imaginative space.

In the mode of attention we call sympathy, one shadow is answered by another.

As a snake moves between sunlight and shade to control the temperature of its blood, there are those whose equilibrium depends on the skill with which they manipulate a crude dialectic.

When the forest returns, all the banished words, kindness, gentleness, innocence, shade, will again be spoken.

A shadow is company, sitting by the fire.

From a slight redistribution of shadows on a face, we infer the arrival of humour, anger, astonishment, pain.

That there are no autonomous facts or events should be an article of faith.

With mosses, lichens, webs and shadows, the goldcrest weaves its nest.

Lying down in the shade, it is easy to forget, to fall into that receptivity upon which memory must cast its image, but a more difficult state to maintain is that forgetfulness on which no image is thrown.

There is no shadow with enough density to impede a song, no song with enough weight to bend a willow branch.

In secret places, under alders, by slow-moving streams, the torn fabric of quiet is quietly repaired.

To avoid the scrutiny of light, forms in shade are constantly changing – mist into smoke, fox into scent, girl into laurel.

The fluidity of flute notes, where they weave among the beech trunks, is impeded by a melancholy, the initiative each note savours before lending itself to the melody.

Accepting an invitation, or ignoring a warning, we step into the shadows.

The coolness which the shadow spreads at the foot of the tree is a detachment not to be confused with indifference.

That which is most intimate to us comes and goes like a shadow and is the gift of light which is continually arriving from a great distance.

I can remember as a child, crossing a field in Ireland, wondering if my shadow would ever be as big as the shadow of my grandfather.

I can remember, on a straight road in Italy, after several days of walking in the mountains, the contrast between the clarity of my mind and the ragged outline of my shadow.

Shadow falls on shadow, sorrow on sorrow.

In the heat of noon we may come to a place where someone planted long ago an avenue of chestnut trees.

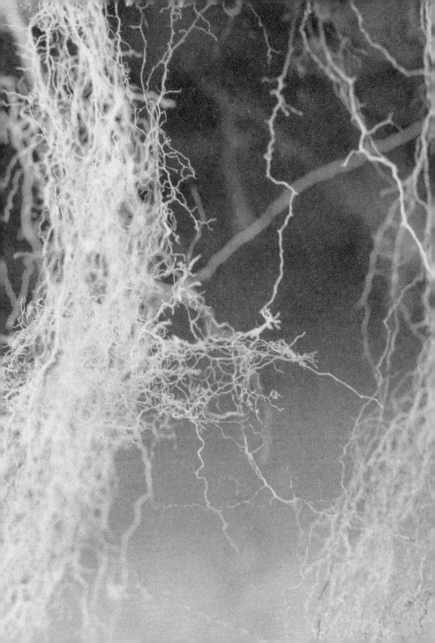

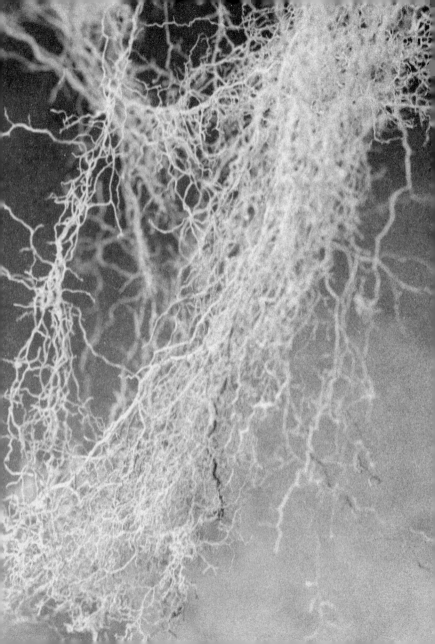

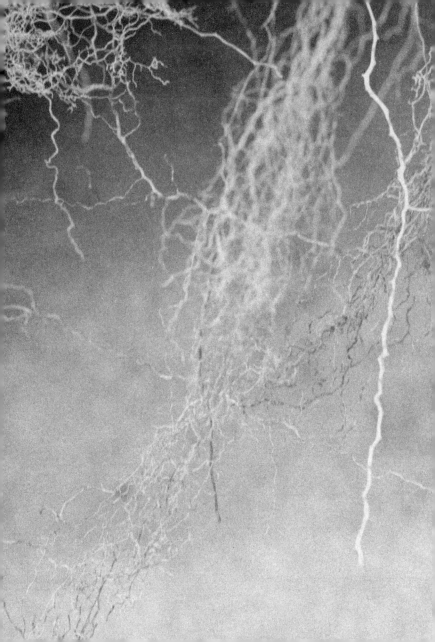

The Blue of Flax

At first glance, it is a strip of colour, intense enough to startle, misplaced among the balanced modulations of green.

Blue, yet not blue, grey, silver, almost white, with a shifting haze of pink; none of these are resolved, as if blue was an aspiration, a syllable you hardly dare to breathe.

A mist rising from the ground, a fallen piece of the sky; these fancies are quickly discarded for the pleasure of the shifting information.

Is it a flax field or is it the sea?

The colour is unstable, weightless, detached from form, a plenitude without presence, not anything you could touch.

Already, at the first glance, before it stretches away, it stretches away, seeking more of itself, more than itself, impatient of any horizon.

Somewhere between milkwort and alkanet, the blue might be located, but these flowers would be darker, less subtle in a mass.

Look closer, the blue of a single flower is deeper than the blue of a field of flowers.

It is, like some faces, concealed or distributed in its openness.

If Bonnard had painted the delicate blue of flax, he would have laid his colour over a white ground.

Since the colour never settles, the gaze cannot settle, but is continually broken into glances that are never swift enough to catch a quality that avoids attention.

The prevarications, the endless qualifications of the writer may be more useful here than the promised fidelity of a painter or photographer.

The thrill of colour is accessory to the fact that it is there, suddenly, in a fold of the hills, taking up the whole of your vision.

If you approach it, day after day, for as long as the flowers are open, you will never overtake this moment of surprise, never quite anticipate the gift of colour.

In a moment, at a glance, you are taken out of your own care.

While lavender fields spread a dusk at noon, in a flax field it is always dawn.

Rippling in the breeze, the flax might be a flag declaring its allegiance to morning, a summons to lyrical adventure.

It is as if, among the hills, a space was cleared for a light but essential joy, or some caprice of the gratuitous.

The field seems larger when the flowers are open and the far edge of the field might almost reach into another country.

A gate leading into a flax field should always be left open.

Where a drift of bluebells will lead farther in, to the half-formed, the deferred, the blue of flax is all external, a supplement or revelation.

Three blue wren's eggs, hidden in a dry stone wall, might be its true counterpart.

The whole period of flowering could be considered a single, unclouded day.

As hope blossoms from fact, the possible within the actual, clarity may have the force of an intimation.

When the blue of flax is over, the distant hills remember.

A Walk by Moonlight

As the last tinge of sunset fades and a flock of geese flies over, the moon rises unscathed from the branches of a hawthorn.

Into an economy of desires, the arrogance of the days, the compromises and complacencies, is introduced a silver light, a delicate stream of irony.

To come out of the house, to come out of yourself, to be subtle, clear, extensive, cold, is the moon's invitation.

You will find a clear path through the beech wood, scented with the leaves of wild garlic and lit by the wild garlic flowers.

Darkness is not closed but open.

The impatience with which we seek the confirmations of light is a flight from information brought by all the senses to the evidence of the eyes alone.

Those objects which by day presented hard surfaces to the light by the light of the moon take on their proper density.

In a yellow rectangle, in the black façade of a house, a woman is laying a table.

Only when you forget the night, when you sleep through it or repress the memory of its distances, will the days appear to be an uninterrupted sequence.

By moonlight, in the far meadow of an old legend, oak trees dance and standing stones walk down to the river to drink.

The lines and limits, the defining edges, which the eye abstracts from a landscape, dissolve and merge by moonlight into masses and tones.

Everything we habitually recognise and dismiss, we are able to meet again.

Walls, trees and hills which all day have kept their distance, at night become presences that gather around.

You can walk out into the moonlight and hear a sonata for piano and oboe.

In ten paces you may come to ten places.

Since trepidation is only a step away from wonder, it is not wrong to hesitate.

When you see a new moon, uncover your head, turn over the penny in your pocket, and lay yourself open for inspection.

Anything that is secretly glad comes under the auspices of the moon.

Constant vigilance would be a parody of attention, a fullness without phases, an inability to put the self to sleep.

Who has the courage to go into the dark places where there is nothing but feeling?

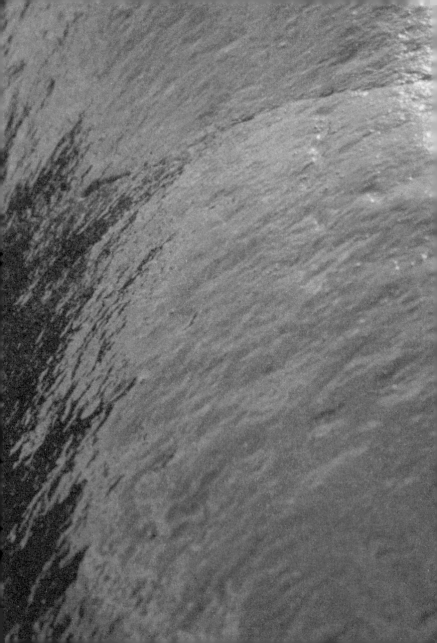

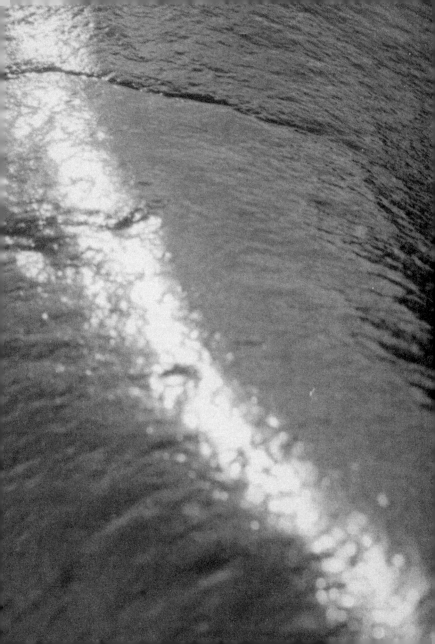

Tobar Na Cailleach

On the hill pass there is a spring where water tumbles out of rock to splash among liverworts and thyme.

A few steps aside from the path, it offers the refreshment of a pause, an excuse to stand at ease and look out over islands.

When you stoop to drink, you are immediately out of the wind, sheltered within a parenthesis of rock, numbed by the rush of water.

The first draught of water burns your throat, as if all the subterranean levels of cold had risen to meet you.

Where you are, who you are: for a moment these questions are shocked into silence.

You can place your lips to the braid of water, plunge your head under, or cool your rock burned hands.

You can splash your face with water and then lift it to the breeze.

This brief contact with another element is enough to separate you from yourself and to return you to yourself again.

After the long walk up the hill, it is good to turn aside, to rest and consider the gentle downhill slope.

In that lonely spot, the sound of water is good company.

Up here, the air is so clear that looking is a kind of tasting.

The distance you have travelled is cancelled at a taste of water.

The keenness of your thirst is answered by the neutrality of water.

Around the well, there is a flush of enriched earth yielding mosses and small flowering plants.

The well is itself a flower nodding in the light, with long roots reaching back into the seams of rock.

If each gesture seems large, here on the open hillside, the taste of water gives a counter measure.

You are not composed of water, hills and air, but you take your place in the conversation of water, hills and air.

An iron cup hangs from a chain but two hands make the best cup for water.

A large boulder belonging to the place is continually soaked with water.

Only one who drinks from the well will know if the water is sweet and cold.

Riasg Buidhe

There are other lives we might lead, places we might get to know, skills we might acquire.

When we have put distance between ourselves and our intentions, the sensibility comes awake.

Every day should contain a pleasure as simple as walking on the machair or singing to the seals.

The ripples on the beach and the veins in the rocks on the mountain show the same signature.

When we climb high enough we can find patches of snow untouched by the sun, parts of the spirit still intact.

The grand landscapes impress us with their weight and scale but it is the anonymous places, a hidden glen or a stretch of water without a name, that steal the heart.

The mere sight of a meadow cranesbill can open up a wound.

We live in an age so completely self-absorbed that the ability to simply look, to pour out the intelligence through the eyes, is an accomplishment.

You will require a tune for a country road, for hill walking a slow air.

When I climb down from the hill I carry strands of wool and fronds of bracken on my clothing, small barbs of quiet in my mind.

At dawn and again at dusk we feel most acutely the passing of time but at dawn the world is with us while at dusk we stand alone.

The farther we move from habitation, the larger are the stars.

There is a kind of bagpipe and fiddle music, practised in a gale, which is full of distance and longing.

A common disease of sheep, the result of cobalt deficiency, is known as 'pine'.

The best amusement in rain is to sit and watch the clouds negotiate the mountain.

Long silences are as proper in good company as a song on a lonely road.

Let everything you do have the clean edge of water lapping in a bay.

In any prevailing wind there are small pockets of quiet: in a rock pool choked with duckweed, in the lee of a cairn, in the rib-cage of a sheep's carcase.

When my stick strikes a stone, it is a call to order.

The most satisfying product of culture is bread.

In a landscape of Torridonian sandstone and heather moor, green and gold lichens on the naked rock will ignite small explosions of sensation.

Whatever there is in a landscape emerges if we just sit still.

It is not from novelty but from an unbroken tradition that real human warmth can be obtained, like a peat fire that has been rekindled continuously for hundreds of years.

After days of walking on the moor, shoulders, spine and calves become as resilient as heather.

The hardest materials are those which display the most obvious signs of weathering.

We can carry a tent, food, clothing or the world on our shoulders, but how light we feel when we lay them down.

Just to look at a beach of grey pebbles can cool the forehead.

On a small island, the feeble purchase that the land obtains between the sea and the sky, the drifting of mist and the intensity of light, unsettles the intellect and opens the imagination to larger and more liquid configurations.

Although the days should extend in a graceful contour, the hours should not be accountable.

A book of poems in the rucksack – that is the relation of art to life.

On a fine day, up on the heights, with heat shimmering from the rocks, I can stretch out on my back and watch all the distances dance.

The duty of the traveller, wherever he finds himself, is always to keep faith with the air.

We should nurture our own loneliness like an Alpine blossom.

Solitude and affection go well together – to work alone the whole day and then in the evening sit round a table with friends.

To meet another person on a walk is like coming to a river.

In the art of the great music, the drone is eternity, the tune tradition, the performance the life of the individual.

It is on bare necessity that lyricism flourishes best, like a cushion of moss campion on granite.

When the people are gone, and the house is a ruin, for long afterwards there may flourish a garden of daffodils.

The routines we accept can strangle us but the rituals we choose give renewed life.

When the lark sings and the air is still, I sometimes feel I could reach over and take the island in my hand like a stone.

Biographical Notes

Thomas A. Clark

Thomas A. Clark was born in Greenock and now lives in Gloucestershire. In recent years, the different landscapes of the Highlands and Islands have been the central preoccupation of his poetry. Since 1986, with the artist Laurie Clark, he has directed Cairn Gallery, one of the earliest and most respected of 'artist-run spaces', specialising in conceptual, minimal and land art, and situated in the small Cotswold town of Nailsworth.

Publications include *A Still Life* (The Jargon Society, North Carolina 1977), *Madder Lake* (Coach House Press, Toronto 1981), *The Tempers of Hazard* (Paladin, London 1993), *Tormentil and Bleached Bones* (Polygon, Edinburgh 1993), *That Which Appears* (Paragon Press, London 1994), *One Hundred Scottish Places* (October, Eindhoven 1999) and numerous small books and cards from his Moschatel Press.

Olwen Shone

Olwen Shone is a graduate of Glasgow School of Art who now lives and works on North Uist. Inspired by the diversities of the island, she makes pictures that are a poetic response to the intimate forms and patterns found in this rural landscape.

The text and images for Distance & Proximity were brought together in September 2000 while Thomas A Clark was poet-in-residence at Taigh Chearsabhagh Arts Centre, Lochmaddy, North Uist.

pocketbooks

Summer 1998

01   GREEN WATERS
      An anthology of boats and voyages, edited by Alec Finlay;
      featuring poetry, prose and visual art by Ian Stephen,
      Ian Hamilton Finlay, Graham Rich.
      ISBN 0 9527669 2 2; paperback, 96pp, colour illustrations, reprinting.

Spring 2000

02   ATOMS OF DELIGHT
      An anthology of Scottish haiku and short poems, edited with an
      Introduction by Alec Finlay, and a Foreword by Kenneth White.
      ISBN 0 7486 6275 8; paperback, 208pp, £7.99.

03   LOVE FOR LOVE
      An anthology of love poems, edited by John Burnside and
      Alec Finlay, with an Introduction by John Burnside.
      ISBN 0 7486 6276 6; paperback, 200pp, £7.99.

04   WITHOUT DAY
      An anthology of proposals for a new Scottish Parliament, edited
      by Alec Finlay, with an Introduction by David Hopkins. *Without
      Day* includes an Aeolus CD by William Furlong.
      ISBN 0 7486 6277 4; paperback with CD, 184pp, £7.99 (including VAT).

Autumn 2000

05   WISH I WAS HERE
An anthology representing the diversity of cultures, languages and dialects in contemporary Scotland, edited by Kevin MacNeil and Alec Finlay, with an Aeolus CD.
ISBN 0 7486 62812 paperback, 208pp, £7.99

06   WILD LIFE
Walks in the Cairngorms. Recording fourteen seven-day walks made by Hamish Fulton between 1985 and 1999, *Wild Life* includes an interview with the artist by Gavin Morrison and an Aeolus CD.
ISBN 0 7486 62820 paperback, 208pp, £7.99

07   GRIP
A new collection of darkly humorous drawings by David Shrigley, *Grip* is the largest collection of Shrigley's work published to date and includes 16 colour illustrations and an Afterword by Patricia Ellis.
ISBN 0 7486 62389 paperback, 208pp, £7.99

Spring 2001

08   DISTANCE & PROXIMITY
The first collection of Scottish poet Thomas A. Clark's prose poems, *Distance & Proximity* includes the ever-popular *In Praise of Walking*, as well as a number of previously unpublished works, accompanied by the suggestive textures of Olwen Shone's photographs.
ISBN 0 7486 6288X paperback, 128pp, £7.99

09   THE WAY TO COLD MOUNTAIN
A Scottish mountains anthology weaving together poetry, nature writing and mountaineering adventures, edited by Alec Finlay, with photographs by David Paterson.
ISBN 0 7486 62898 paperback, 208pp, £7.99

10   THE ORDER OF THINGS
The Order of Things is an anthology of shape and pattern poems that explore the grain of language and imitate the forms of nature. It includes Renaissance pattern poems and contemporary concrete, sound and visual poetry. Edited by Ken Cockburn with Alec Finlay; with anaccompanying CD.
ISBN 0 7486 62901 paperback, 208pp, £7.99

Autumn 2001

11   MACKEREL & CREAMOLA
A collection of Ian Stephen's linked short stories with recipe-poems, illustrated with children's drawings. *Mackerel & Creamola* draws on Stephen's deep knowledge of the Hebrides, sea lore, and his experiences as a coastguard and sailor. With a Foreword by Gerry Cambridge and a CD featuring stories and a dash of harmonica.
ISBN 0 7486 63029 paperback, 208pp, £7.99

12   THE LIBRARIES OF THOUGHT & IMAGINATION
An anthology of 'Bookshelves' selected by artists and writers, and an illustrated survey of artist projects celebrating books and libraries. Edited by Alec Finlay with an Introduction by Colin Sackett, and an Afterword edited by Olaf Nicolai featuring an anthology of imagined books.
ISBN 0 7486 63002 paperback, 208pp, £7.99

13   UNRAVELLING THE RIPPLE
Book Artist Helen Douglas a beautiful and striking portrait of the tideline on a Hebridean island. Published in full colour, *Unravelling the Ripple* unfolds as a single image that flows through the textures and rhythms of sand, sea-wrack, rock and wave, to reveal dynamic sensual and imaginative depths.
ISBN 0 7486 63037 paperback, 208pp, £7.99

Spring 2002

Available through all good bookshops.

Book trade orders to:
Scottish Book Source, 137 Dundee Street, Edinburgh EH11 1BG.

Copies are also available from:
Morning Star Publications, Canongate Venture (5), New Street,
Edinburgh EH8 8BH.

Website: www.pbks.co.uk